THE FAST WAY TO FATHER OF THE BRIDE'S SPEECH

BULLET GUIDE

Matt Avery

Hodder Education, 338 Euston Road, London NW1 3BH

Hodder Education is an Hachette UK company

First published in UK 2011 by Hodder Education

This edition published 2011

Copyright © 2011 Matt Avery

The moral rights of the author have been asserted

Database right Hodder Education (makers)

Artworks (internal and cover): Peter Lubach
Cover concept design: Two Associates

British Library Cataloguing in Publication Data: a catalogue record for this title is available from the British Library.

10 9 8 7 6 5 4 3 2 1

The publisher has used its best endeavours to ensure that any website addresses referred to in this book are correct and active at the time of going to press. However, the publisher and the author have no responsibility for the websites and can make no guarantee that a site will remain live or that the content will remain relevant, decent or appropriate.

The publisher has made every effort to mark as such all words which it believes to be trademarks. The publisher should also like to make it clear that the presence of a word in the book, whether marked or unmarked, in no way affects its legal status as a trademark.

Every reasonable effort has been made by the publisher to trace the copyright holders of material in this book. Any errors or omissions should be notified in writing to the publisher, who will endeavour to rectify the situation for any reprints and future editions.

Hachette UK's policy is to use papers that are natural, renewable and recyclable products and made from wood grown in sustainable forests. The logging and manufacturing processes are expected to conform to the environmental regulations of the country of origin.

www.hoddereducation.co.uk

Typeset by Stephen Rowling/Springworks

Printed in Spain

To all the parents

Acknowledgements

My sincere thanks to everyone who contributed to this book with details of their experiences; and to those whose support made it possible, especially my family, Victoria at Hodder Education, and Suze.

About the author

Matt Avery trained as an actor and speech and drama practitioner. He has spent the last 20 years training people in public speaking for all manner of occasions, private and corporate, as well as practising what he preaches at his own wedding – and other people's!

In addition to lecturing in motivational speaking, Matt runs group coaching sessions for anyone who will be a speaker at a forthcoming wedding and who would like some expert guidance.

Please visit perfectweddingspeechesfast.com for more information.

Contents

Introduction

Your daughter's wedding is without doubt one of the **biggest days in her life** – and one of the biggest days in yours. It's a momentous and joyful occasion, and yet for many a father of the bride it's a day that is significantly marred by one thing: the **looming dread** of having to stand up in front of assembled family and friends to give their speech.

You're bound to be feeling the **pressure** of getting your speech just right. This can be enough to ensure that it's at the back of your mind throughout the day until you've got it over with. By that time you'll have missed out on enjoying the build-up, the ceremony, the arrival at the reception venue and the wedding breakfast.

Shouldn't you be able to **enjoy giving your speech** rather than just trying to get through it with your dignity intact and your lunch still in your stomach? What if it was something you actually looked forward to doing?

By **preparing thoroughly** – fully understanding what's involved and how you are likely to feel on the day – you can turn giving your speech from something you endure into something you relish. By writing your speech carefully and perfecting its delivery, learning how to control your nerves (and even use them to your advantage) and getting your audience relaxed and on your side, your speech can become a highlight of your day and a **cherished memory** for your daughter.

This book shows you how.

'There are only two types of speakers in the world – 1. The nervous and 2. Liars.'

Mark Twain

1 So, you have to make a speech?

'Unaccustomed as I am...'

Whether or not you are used to public speaking, giving the father of the bride's speech at your daughter's wedding is something for which you need to prepare specifically. It's of **huge importance**, both to you and to your daughter, and something at which you only get one chance.

You therefore simply have to get it right first time. **Prepare your speech thoroughly**, however, and you can enjoy it too.

● Your daughter is depending on you to give a great speech…

This chapter highlights the **most important elements** to concentrate on when you know you're going to have to make the speech:

* initial preparations
* the first six things to do right now
* your role on the day
* consulting the bride and groom
* when you will need to give your speech
* the people you will have to thank and toast.

You have to get it right first time

Initial preparations

Whether you are a seasoned veteran of public speaking or this will be your first time, some key factors will **set this occasion apart**.

* It will be one of the most **important** speeches you'll ever give.
* The sense of occasion will add to the **pressure.**
* You'll feel **responsible** to your daughter and her new husband to do it well.
* You'll be in front of **family and friends,** who may be:
  » supportive
  » quick to tease if it all goes wrong!
* You'll be delivering your speech to a large number of people whose **opinions matter** to you.

However, the good news is that effective public speaking is something that anyone can learn.

'Proper planning and preparation prevent poor performance.'
Charlie Batch

It's never too early to start

When it comes to your wedding speech, there is no such thing as being over-prepared. **Take your time** to decide what you want to say, so that you are happy with the content of your speech.

Getting yourself **organized early** is important because it will help to:

* settle your **nerves**
* ensure that you don't **omit** anything important
* ensure that you don't **ad-lib** anything that you later regret
* give you the time and opportunity to **rehearse** your speech.

● Give yourself plenty of time to prepare your speech

Top tip
Prepare well, and prepare early!

The six things to do right now

You can accomplish the following six things right now. Achieving them will:

* help focus your mind on the task ahead
* prepare the necessary groundwork.

1 Begin sketching out a **draft plan** of your speech – however rough.
2 Ask the happy couple whether they want to be **consulted** on your speech.
3 Consult with **your partner** and other **family members** for additional material.
4 Know who is being invited so that you can **pitch** your speech appropriately.
5 Start practising **speaking out loud** – and loudly – whenever you're on your own.
6 Line up some willing **volunteers** who can listen to you practise making your speech.

Top tip
Keep your draft speech with you at all times, so that you can regularly and easily update it.

Your role on the day

Your daughter's wedding day should be one of the happiest in her life. You can help ensure that it is by properly understanding what will be required of you:

Before the ceremony	During the ceremony	After the ceremony
Be fully aware of the day's timetable and make sure everyone keeps to it	Walk into the venue with your daughter's arm linked in yours	Socialize with your guests
Settle your daughter's nerves en route to the venue	Take responsibility for the pace as you enter the venue – walk slowly and steadily	Try to cater for everyone's needs
Remind her that you are delighted in her choice of husband	Deliver your daughter to the groom's side before taking your seat	Act as diplomat and peacemaker if necessary
Tell her how beautiful she looks	Remember to smile!	Deliver your speech brilliantly!

Consulting the bride and groom

Ask your daughter and her fiancé whether they wish your speech to:

* be a **complete surprise** on the day
* have an **agreed** tone and content
* be written in **conjunction** with them.

You may have a preference, but determining theirs is a great way to:

* make them feel **included**
* find out about their expectations
* **avoid** any regrets over inclusions or omissions to your speech
* **reassure** them that there won't be any nasty surprises.

> The speeches are the one part of the wedding day that don't traditionally involve the bride. Consulting your daughter on your speech is a great opportunity to make her feel included.

'Now join hands, and with your hands your hearts.'

William Shakespeare

8

Your prospective son-in-law

You'll need to talk with **authority** (and with **affection**!) about your new **son-in-law,** so you'll need to know some **relevant details** about him. These include:

* how he and your daughter met
* interesting background information (his interests, hobbies, skills, achievements, etc.)
* any amusing anecdotes that would be relevant.

Most of your speech should come from your **own experiences,** but additional research will help to make your speech much **more rounded**.

Saying the wrong thing
Since you don't know your new son-in-law's entire history it's all too easy to upset someone by saying the wrong thing. It's far better to err on the side of caution.

When to give your speech

Traditionally, there are **three wedding speeches**.
They occur in the following order:

1 father of the bride's speech
2 groom's speech
3 best man's speech.

Your speech will therefore come **first**. This means
that it will need to:

* begin with a welcome to your guests
* put your guests at ease and break the ice
* end with a handover to your son-in-law.

It also means that you get to enjoy the other
speeches, with yours 'in the bag'!

● It's good to go first...

Your speech will come first

Whom to thank and toast

It is traditional for the father of the bride to thank people and to propose a toast. You can offer the thanks and toast on **behalf** of **yourself** and **your partner**, if appropriate. Remember that it's **not traditional** for the father of the bride to present **gifts**.

You must thank:

* your **guests** for joining you on your daughter and her new husband's special day
* all those guests who have come a **long way**
* **any special guests**.

You must propose a toast to:

* the health and happiness of the **bride and groom**.

You may also wish to **compliment** your **daughter** on the way she looks and congratulate your new **son-in-law**.

Top tip
Before you begin, have your glass at the ready for the toast.

2 Writing your speech: the basics

The perfect wedding speech

You don't need to be a professional speech-writer to write the **perfect** wedding speech. To make it **meaningful** it needs to be **personal**. Cherry-picking material from sample speeches will only result in a bland speech that could be given by any father about any bride and groom, to any audience.

By thinking about **what you want to say,** structuring your thoughts carefully and continually refining them as time goes by, you'll find that everyone can write a **great wedding speech**.

● Think carefully about what you want to say…

Your advantage, as father of the bride, is that your audience will be greatly looking forward to your speech, and willing you to do well.

This chapter covers the **basic points** you need to consider. It tells you how to:

* start and finish strongly
* decide what to say
* structure your speech
* decide how long it should be
* set the tone – sentimental or humorous?
* meet audience expectations
* represent your partner
* personalize your speech.

Everyone can write a great wedding speech

Starting and finishing strongly

The beginning and end of your speech are the parts most likely to be remembered, so it is crucial to make sure that these are **really strong**.

A strong start will:	A strong finish will:
grab your audience's attention	bring your speech to a definite conclusion
help them relax (which will help you relax!)	ensure a smooth handover to the groom
break the ice	leave on a high note
make them want to listen to your speech.	leave the audience wanting more.

Top tip

If you suggest that the groom and best man will soon be 'entertaining us', this will take the pressure off you to 'entertain'. Sincerity is the key.

What should I say?

Besides offering the essential thanks and toast (see chapter 1), this is your opportunity to **sing your daughter's praises** and warmly, and publicly, **welcome your new son-in-law** to the family. How you do this largely depends on:

* how you want to come across
* what you feel comfortable expressing.

However, the golden rule is to make sure your speech revolves around the happy couple. You could consider:

* relating an **anecdote** about when you **first met** your son-in-law
* recounting an amusing **incident** from your daughter's childhood
* saying how **proud** you are of your daughter
* stating how **pleased** you (and your partner) are for your **daughter** and **son-in-law**.

Remember
Any anecdotes must be kind, unembarrassing and relevant.

Structuring your speech

A good approach is to **divide** your speech into **sections** so that it takes your audience on a **journey**. For example:

Top tip
Try to ensure that your speech **flows** from one section to the next.

1 **Welcome** your guests and **thank** them for joining you (and your partner) on this **special day**.

2 **Express** your **feelings** about:
   » your **daughter** getting married
   » your new **son-in-law**.

3 **Tell** the audience about how you have struck up a **friendship** with the **groom's parents**.

4 **Describe** your **daughter** and how **beautiful** she looks.

5 Thank your **partner** for their **support**.

6 Conclude with a **handover** to the **groom**.

18

How long should it be?

The speeches are a part of the day to which most guests look forward. However, it is good to remember that:

A **short** speech…

✔ will be more **memorable**
✔ will leave the audience **wanting** more
✔ might be a **pleasant surprise!**

A **long** speech…

✘ may make the audience **restless**
✘ can appear **self-indulgent**
✘ is **unfair** to the **speakers** still to come.

'Always be shorter than anybody dared to hope.'
Lord Reading

Remember
Your speech will not exist in isolation. Your audience will have another two speeches to listen to after yours, so be aware that less is more. Any audience has a maximum tolerance for listening!

Setting the tone

When you are writing your speech, it's important to consider how you want to come across to your audience; it's not simply about how it sounds to you. Yours will be the **first** speech and your audience will be:

* expectant
* nervous on your behalf.

You therefore have **two primary objectives** in establishing the **right note**:

1 to put your audience **at ease** – if they relax and are confident in your abilities it will help you relax and help them to enjoy your speech
2 to set an **appropriate** tone for the content of your speech – you should aim to create **early on** an atmosphere of:
   a love
   b warmth
   c happiness
   d joy
   e pride.

'They may forget what you said, but they will never forget how you made them feel.'

Carl W. Buechner

20

Audience expectations

Your audience will have some **predetermined** expectations of your speech. They will **expect** you to be:

✔ *sincere in what you say about your daughter*
✔ *loving towards her and your new son-in-law*
✔ *warm and affectionate in tone and content.*

They will **not expect** you to be:

✘ *hugely entertaining*
✘ *overly sentimental*
✘ *telling embarrassing stories about your daughter*
✘ *dropping any kind of bombshell.*

● Don't drop any bombshells!

Remember
In addition to their expectations, your audience will be grateful if you're not long-winded!

Create an atmosphere of love and pride

Representing your partner

If you have a partner your speech should not represent **you in isolation**, but should represent your partner too. If you discuss the speech with your partner beforehand, you can ensure that it:

* reflects their thoughts, wishes and sentiments
* encompasses how you both feel
* includes any additional material they may want conveyed.

Top tip
Make sure that you refer to your partner throughout your speech so that it's clear that you're speaking on their behalf too.

Your partner's speech
If your partner is going to say a few words too, your speech need not represent them. Try instead to ensure that the two speeches dovetail – and avoid any repetition.

Personalizing the speech

The **last thing you want** is to deliver a speech that could have been given by any father of the bride, about any happy couple. Every bride and groom are **different**, and so is every father of the bride – so use this to your **advantage**. Guests may:

1 know the groom
2 know the bride
3 know them both
4 not know either of them (e.g. some guests' partners).

> **Remember**
> Your speech should be personal and come from your feelings and memories, but done with a light touch.

This gives you the perfect opportunity to **vary** your speech to **accommodate everyone** – while making it **personal** to the bride and groom. Try to:

* describe your relationship with the groom
* describe your relationship with your daughter
* introduce them both to those who don't know them.

3 Writing your speech: advanced techniques

From a good speech to a great speech

To give your speech the **extra sparkle** that will elevate it above and beyond the majority of speeches and make it **truly memorable,** you will need to employ some more advanced speech-writing techniques. These will enable you to change a good speech into a great speech.

Through a process of **enhancements** and **fine tuning**, you will lift your speech to the next level. You will also need to be careful to negotiate any **potential controversy** or faux pas.

● Be prepared to go through a number of drafts to get to that great speech!

A great speech does not have to be complicated, but to be really successful it should **charm** and **fascinate** your audience. You want such an important part of the wedding celebration to be recalled fondly for a long time afterwards.

This chapter focuses on the following advanced techniques:

* fine tuning
* conveying emotion
* using humour
* using anecdotes
* injecting variety

* words of wisdom
* avoiding controversy and faux pas
* dealing with awkward set-ups.

Lift your speech to the next level

Fine tuning

Be prepared to **revise** your speech often, **crafting** it until you've smoothed off all the rough edges and removed any waffle. Try to get into the habit of **updating** it on a regular basis, particularly:

* after presenting it to anyone who is helping you practise
* after adding new material (check for repetition)
* after not looking at it for a few days (to gain perspective).

At the very least you should aim to revise your speech **once a week**. Consult the other speech givers too, to make sure that you are not repeating anything they have planned to say.

Remember
Great speeches aren't written; they're rewritten!

'If you can't write your message in a sentence, you can't say it in an hour.'
Dianna Booher

28

Conveying emotion

It's important to strike the right **balance** between writing a speech that is dry and dispassionate and one that gushes with emotion.

Too much emotion may:

* be embarrassing for the people listening
* make the happy couple feel awkward
* get in the way of what you're trying to say.

If there is **too little emotion**, you may:

* seem disinterested
* appear heartless
* come across as cold or unfeeling.

Top tip

Test the reaction of your 'practice audience'. If they are embarrassed listening to your speech, even if it's just one section, you need to change it to avoid the possibility of embarrassing everyone on the day.

Using humour

Adding some humour to your speech can be a great way to:

* **break** the ice
* add **variety**
* help you **relax**
* help **everyone else** relax.

> You will need to ensure that the humorous and serious elements are carefully balanced so that your speech doesn't appear flippant.

Try interspersing the more serious sections of your speech with humour. By interweaving the two, the humour will aid the serious moments by:

* making them stand out
* giving them more gravitas
* providing some light relief.

However, be careful not to overdo the jokes – remember that a little humour goes a long way.

A little humour goes a long way

Using anecdotes

Anecdotes can be a great way to **introduce** key members of the wedding party, particularly the bride and groom, to guests who may not know them well – or even at all.

Most of the wedding guests will know either the bride or groom but not necessarily both of them.

Using an anecdote allows you to convey:

* something of their **character**
* an insight into their **personalities**
* interesting **background information**.

Crucially, using **well-chosen** anecdotes means that you can achieve all this in a way that is:

* fun
* entertaining
* accessible.

Top tip
Relating an anecdote about yourself and the groom can be a great way to break the ice and help you relax.

Injecting variety

Your speech will typically be one of three, so it's a good idea to inject some variety into it. Suitable ways to achieve this include:

* using props
* showing slides
* playing music.

Adding variety helps to keep your speech **fresh** and will **differentiate** it from the other speeches. It also:

* creates interest for those listening
* breaks up your speech
* divides your speech into sections.

Remember
Use only things that are **directly relevant** to your speech, and that support or embellish it.

Top tip
Be careful not to overdo it! If your entire speech is filled with props, slides and music this ceases to add variety.

Words of wisdom

It can be a **lovely gesture** for the father of the bride to offer some words of wisdom to the happy couple. These words can be poignant or humorous.

Try to make sure that any advice you give isn't of an **intimate or personal** nature and doesn't seem **condescending**. Make sure that what you say is:

* true and accurate
* appropriate to the occasion
* helpful and relevant
* food for thought for their future.

Collective wisdom
It's often a good idea not to rely solely on your own experiences to provide insight, but to use the collective wisdom of generations of married couples. The internet is invaluable for researching information of this kind.

Avoiding controversy and faux pas

To ensure that the day **runs smoothly**, it's essential to avoid any faux pas. Crucial to this is thorough **research**. By learning as much as you can about your new son-in-law and his family, and any relevant sensibilities, you're well placed to avoid any **subject areas** that may be **sensitive** to them.

Try to **make sure** you:

✔ understand the relationship complexities of all parties
✔ ensure that your speech is:
  » tactful
  » diplomatic
✔ err on the side of caution.

Don't:

✘ include any material you're not sure about
✘ be tempted to improvise
✘ take unnecessary risks.

'Grasp the subject, the words will follow.'
Cato The Elder

Top tip
Don't mention any of the bride's or groom's **previous partners**!

34

Dealing with awkward set-ups

Challenging or difficult family set-ups must be handled with **tact** and **diplomacy**. First, identify any potentially awkward scenarios.

Absent family or friends might be:	The bride or groom might have:
deceased	children
military personnel serving overseas	been married previously
in prison.	been previously engaged to one of the guests.

Any awkwardness can be overcome by using the **REDS** acronym:

1 **R**esearch – what's the **situation**?
2 **E**nquiry – how would **interested parties** like the situation to be handled?
3 **D**etermine your course of **action**
4 **S**tick to it.

● Be prepared to play piggy in the middle

4 Practising your speech

Practice makes perfect

We all know that 'practice makes perfect' and, if you're unused to public speaking, it's especially important to familiarize yourself with your speech and its delivery.

By practising your speech, you will grow in **confidence** while **honing your technique** to ensure that you make the **most of the occasion**.

Don't feel you need to wait until your speech is written completely before you start practising – the sooner you start, the better!

● Practise, practise, practise… anywhere, any time!

When practising your speech, think about what you are saying and how you would like to say it, and consider your **posture** and **body language** too. You can use a range of **techniques** when you practise. This chapter explains how important it is to:

* memorize your key points
* find your style
* make the mirror your best friend
* learn to stand still
* say it out loud
* rehearse in front of other people
* project the best 'you'
* exude confidence.

The sooner you start, the better

Memorizing your key points

Good **speech delivery** is a skill that needs to be learned and practised. The aim is not to be able to repeat the words verbatim, but to learn the content thoroughly enough to be able to memorize your key points. This will help you sound natural and feel relaxed.

The amount of practice you'll need to put in will depend on a number of factors, including your:

* previous **experience**
* natural **aptitude**
* level of **confidence**.

> **Remember**
> Repetition through practice will not only improve your delivery but also help you control your nerves.

However, no matter what your starting position, the more practice you put in the better your speech will be. So practise early and practise often.

Finding your style

Use your preparation time as an opportunity to try out different ways of delivering your speech. When you find the style that suits you best, keep practising to refine and improve your delivery. A good way to edit your delivery is to record yourself delivering your speech.

As the saying goes, the more you put in the more you get out. As you become familiar with your speech, your confidence level will increase proportionately. As you gain in confidence, you will:

* start to feel more **relaxed**
* slow down your **delivery**
* begin to **enjoy** giving your speech.

'It's not necessarily the amount of time you spend at practice that counts; it's what you put into the practice.'

Eric Lindros

Making the mirror your best friend

Practise your speech standing in front of a **full-length mirror**. Do you:

1 **shuffle** your feet?
2 **fidget**?
3 feel **self-conscious**?

By watching yourself, you can see and help to eradicate any **distracting habits** you may have while building your **confidence** and losing your **inhibitions**.

● The mirror can be a vital tool for self-presentation… and calming those nerves!

Top tip
Check your body language and watch out for potentially off-putting tics or mannerisms.

Learning to stand still

One of the most obvious **giveaways** of a nervous speaker or an under-rehearsed speech is someone **shuffling** their feet. Most people who do this (and that's most people!) don't even realize they're doing it.

To see if it applies to you, practise in front of:

1 a mirror

2 an invited audience.

If you shuffle, try imagining:	This will help you:
your feet are pinned to the floor	keep your feet firmly planted
a piece of string attached to the top of your head pulling you up.	keep yourself centred.

The result will be that you will stand still, which will help to:

* keep everyone **focused**
* make you look **confident**
* improve your **posture**
* enhance your **delivery**.

Saying it out loud

Most people are **rarely conscious** of hearing their **own voice** in everyday situations, but when it's the only sound in the room and everyone is listening to you, you'll hear it in a whole **new way**. It's something you'll have to get used to, so you will need to practise saying your speech out loud.

If you're not used to public speaking, you'll be amazed how odd your voice sounds at first. Try speaking out loud whenever you're on your own. This will:

* force you to **concentrate** on your **voice**
* give you an **opportunity** to get used to **hearing yourself**
* allow you to **experiment** with pace, pitch and tone
* make it seem **normal**!

Get used to hearing yourself

Top tip
Try the vocal warm-up exercises in chapter 6 before saying your speech out loud.

Rehearsing in front of other people

Practising your speech in front of an audience is **vital preparation** for the big day. You can start with just one person and build up to a few family members or close friends. Initially, you may feel:

* nervous
* awkward
* embarrassed
* self-conscious.

These feelings are entirely **natural,** but they will subside with practice and experience, leaving you free to **enjoy giving** your speech. It's far better to get over this hurdle now than face it for the first time on the big day.

Ask your rehearsal audience the following questions:

☐ Am I speaking clearly?
☐ Am I projecting effectively?
☐ Do I sound tense?

Top tip
The more you practise, the easier it gets.

'Train hard, fight easy.'
Aleksandr Suvorov

Projecting the best 'you'

When you stand up to make your speech your guests become your audience. What is the **first impression** you want them to have of you?

✗ *Nervous*
✗ *Dreading having to give your speech*
✗ *Worried you're going to make a fool of yourself*
✗ *Can't wait to **get it over with**.*

✓ *Confident*
✓ *In control*
✓ *Pleased to be there*
✓ *Looking forward to giving your speech.*

The truth is that, no matter how you feel inside, the audience will only perceive what you project to them.

> **Remember**
> A swan may be paddling furiously below the water, but if on the surface it appears perfectly calm and composed no one will know.

Learning to exude confidence

Feeling confident is great, but you need to **exude** that confidence so that your audience will:

* feel in **safe hands**
* **relax**
* be free to concentrate on what you're saying.

'If you hear a voice within you say "you cannot paint," then by all means paint, and that voice will be silenced.'

Vincent Van Gogh

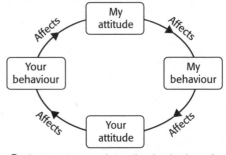

● The Betari Box – the cycle of attitude and behaviour

Remember
How you make your audience feel will directly affect how they make you feel, as the diagram shows.

5 Getting ready for the big day

Things to do in advance

It's vital to get yourself suitably prepared for the big day well in advance, both practically and psychologically. By doing so, you will leave yourself free to enjoy the wedding day to the full.

Nearer the time, it will help you relax if you have familiarized yourself with the **venue**, the **set-up** and the **practicalities** of your speech giving. Then there will be nothing to stop you delivering your speech to the best of your abilities.

● Getting everything done can be a bit of a marathon… but it will be worth it

It's a good idea to make a list of the things you should do well before the day itself. This chapter offers tips on:

* checking out the venue
* practising your speech *in situ*
* using a microphone
* making cue cards
* preparing props.

This chapter also gives you **strategies** for how to overcome **unexpected** situations. Unforeseen scenarios have the potential to ruin your speech (or worse), so consider these possibilities and make plans for dealing with them.

Enjoy the wedding day to the full

Checking out the venue

The excitement of the day, and its significance and importance, will provide quite enough pressure without adding an unnecessary element of surprise. This is why it's essential to know exactly where you will be giving your speech.

Try to visit the wedding venue at least once before the day itself, to familiarize yourself with the room in which you'll be giving your speech. When you get there, take note of:

1 **where** you'll be standing to give your speech
2 the **size** of the room
3 the **acoustics** of the room
4 the **location** and **orientation** of the audience.

Top tip
Visit the venue when it's not busy so that you have the place to yourself to practise your speech.

* Find out whether you will just stand up and speak from your **place at the table** or whether you will have to walk to a **pre-arranged spot**. If it's the latter:
  » make sure the groom knows how **your speech finishes** so he can get ready to follow you
  » determine the **distance** you'll need to cover so you're there in **good time**
  » identify potential **obstacles that could get in your way**.
* If you're using **props**, find somewhere to **store** them.

'Well begun is half done.'
Aristotle

● Identify obstacles that could get in your way

Practising your speech *in situ*

Nothing beats the experience of practising your speech in the **actual venue** in which your daughter's wedding reception will be held. This will do wonders for your **confidence**, knowing that:

- it won't be a surprise on the day
- having done it once you can do it again
- next time you'll be surrounded by encouraging friends and family.

If you can repeat this practice on **several occasions** you'll begin to concentrate on:

- ✔ *what you're saying*
- ✔ *how you're saying it*
- ✔ *how it's coming across*
- ✘ *rather than focusing on how you* ***feel****.*

Top tip

Take someone with you to provide an **audience**. This will add **realism** and provide an opportunity for **feedback** and checking sound levels.

Using a microphone effectively

Even if you feel you don't need one because you have a **loud voice**, unless the venue is quite intimate it's often best to use a microphone. This will:

1 take the **pressure off** you having to project
2 make you sound more **relaxed**, **confident** and **in control**
3 allow more **vocal expression** and subtlety
4 allow you to continue over any **interruptions**.

How to hold it	Where to hold it	How to speak into it
In a comfortable open fist, making sure you don't obscure the mesh	With the top of the microphone just in front of your chin	Speaking normally, keeping your voice at a constant volume

It's often best to use a microphone

Making cue cards

While it's obviously a good idea to be as familiar with your speech as possible, learning it by rote and delivering it **without notes** is a recipe for **disaster**. The pressure of the day can make even the surest memory go blank. Instead, write **brief notes** on **cue cards** to **prompt** you for each section of your speech. It's best to…

* start each new thought on a separate line
* use smart, blank cards with plain backs
* choose cards:
    » small enough to fit in your hand
    » big enough for writing you can read easily.

'Keep your words soft and tender because tomorrow you may have to eat them.'

Anon.

● Cue cards will prompt you for each part of your speech

Preparing props and slides

If you've decided to **liven up** your speech with props or **audio-visual elements,** it's best to prepare these as early as possible. Doing so will give you time to:

✔ *practise with them*
✔ *make sure you know how they all **work***
✔ *work them **seamlessly** into your delivery*
✔ *make sure you can get **everything** you need.*

If you're using **technical** items (such as sound, lighting or slides), be sure to check that:

☐ there will be a **power** outlet to hand
☐ you know how long they take to warm up
☐ you have a **back-up plan** if they fail to work.

Top tip
Using additional and unexpected elements to complement your speech can provide an **extra dimension** and add **variety**.

Unexpected problems

It might sound negative to try to imagine everything that could possibly go wrong, but it's worth it to **pre-empt problems**.

* Think through the whole of your speech, from the moment you place any props or presents to the moment you sit down after a job well done.

> Prevention is better than cure.

* Look at each moment and envisage as many different **challenging scenarios** as possible, and don't be afraid to think **outside the box**…

CASE STUDY: Back-up benefit

'I'd planned to use my laptop to play a recording of my daughter. For some reason it just wouldn't play. Fortunately, I had a back-up sound system set up in advance…'

58

Dealing with 'What if?' scenarios

Once you've identified the possible problems that might occur, you need to think them through in turn and devise a **coping strategy** for dealing with each one. It also helps to think of an **alternative** in case the first is unsuccessful or insufficient.

What if...	Coping strategy	Last resort
...I lose my cue cards?	Make sure you have a spare set (if possible already at the venue)	Make sure another guest has an additional spare set
...someone persistently heckles?	Have a joke prepared to diffuse the situation	Ensure you've primed someone to have a quiet word!
...I forget a key prop?	Have a spare already in place	Have prepared a way to communicate the idea without the prop

6 Dealing with nerves

The fear within

First things first – it's okay to be nervous. In fact, it's actually good to be nervous. Why? Because when you're nervous, your body floods your system with adrenalin, which gives you an all-important **edge**. This edge will make you more alert and energetic, enabling you to deliver your speech with **power**, **passion** and **clarity**.

The trick is to learn to **harness** the adrenalin and use it to your advantage when you deliver your speech.

● We all get nervous …

This chapter explains why it's normal to be nervous before a public performance, and how to accept this as **nature's way** of getting you ready for the task ahead. It offers tips for using your pre-speech nerves to your advantage, and also tells you about:

* why it's important to release tension
* simple relaxation techniques
* confidence 'tricks of the trade'
* the importance of a good warm-up
* two-minute warm-ups that you can do anywhere.

It's okay to be nervous

Why it's good to be nervous

Everyone gets nervous before they have to speak in public. Not only is it perfectly natural, but it's also necessary. Your body is preparing you for a performance that you know is important.

Symptoms you might experience

☐ Heart racing
☐ Wobbly legs
☐ 'Butterflies' in the stomach
☐ Sweating

☐ Shaking hands
☐ Dry mouth
☐ Nausea
☐ Loss of appetite

How these can help you

* Nervousness releases adrenalin into your system, providing you with energy.
* Your body is being supercharged, ready to give a great performance.

Remember
Being nervous is good, but looking nervous isn't, so use the relaxation techniques described in this chapter to help overcome this.

Channelling your adrenalin

Take these steps to make your nervous energy work for you:

✔ *Practise your speech in front of other people.*
✔ *Learn to recognize the feelings you experience when you're nervous.*
✔ **Remind yourself** *that being nervous is a good thing.*

*It's **your body** giving you an **edge**, heightening your **senses** and your **speed of thought** ready to deliver your speech to **maximum effect**.*

*Tell me again why feeling this **bad** is a **good thing**?*

PANIC

BUTTON

● No need to panic!

Why it's important to release tension

Even people who speak professionally experience nerves to some extent before giving a speech, so it's not surprising that most **non-professional public speakers** will feel some anxiety. It is important to try to **relax**, however, to rid your body – and your voice – of tension.

Tension in your body will:

* make you look nervous
* make you want to fidget
* impair your breathing.

Tension in your voice will:

* make you sound nervous
* make you sound strained
* make it difficult to control.

Being relaxed therefore reduces your fear and puts you in control of the situation.

> ## 'If nerves are a public speaker's best friend, tension is his worst enemy.'
> David Windham

Simple relaxation techniques

The following exercises can be done individually or as a group.

Symptom	Exercise	Result
Tightness in shoulders	Shrug tightly, then relax. Repeat. Move shoulders in large circles	No visible tension
Tight voice	Yawn as widely as possible, and vocalize with an 'ahhh' sound	Voice does not sound strained
Shortness of breath	Breathe deeply, hold for ten seconds, breathe out and relax. Repeat	Sound relaxed and in control
Tightness in neck	Circle head slowly in a large arc, in both directions	Relaxed throat – improved vocal quality
Butterflies in stomach; general nervousness	Clench and relax different muscle groups in turn	Less nervousness
Clenched jaw	Swing jaw from side to side, first with mouth open, then closed	Relaxed jaw, allowing the sound out freely

Confidence tricks

Here are some 'tricks of the trade' that professional public speakers use to give them an air of confidence.

- ✔ Know your speech **thoroughly** – and stick to it
- ✔ Have a glass of water to hand
- ✘ Don't drink **alcohol** to calm your nerves – use the **relaxation techniques** instead
- ✔ Fight the temptation to rush your speech:
  - » speak **slowly**
  - » don't forget to **pause**
- ✔ Undo your **top button** (hidden behind cravat/tie)
- ✔ Pick out **one person** at a time and **deliver** that part of the speech **directly** to them
- ✔ Keep your **feet** still
- ✘ Don't speak over **laughter**

Top tip
Remember these tricks to appear calm, confident and relaxed – even if you're not. Don't forget that your audience really wants to hear what you have to say.

The importance of a good warm-up

Don't underestimate the importance of a thorough warm-up. Not only will it **relieve tension and help you feel calm** but it will also **prepare you, physically** and **mentally,** for the task ahead.

Warming up your body will:

* help you relax
* release pent-up adrenalin
* help prevent you shaking
* get rid of any 'wobbly' feelings
* put you in control.

Warming up your voice will:

* make it clearer
* allow everyone to hear you
* make you sound relaxed
* reduce hoarseness
* prevent strain.

Remember
Professional actors always warm up before a performance – and so should you.

A thorough warm-up will prepare you for the task ahead

Physical warm-ups

These two-minute exercises will help you warm up your body, **releasing tension** in preparation for making your speech. You can perform them **anywhere, very quickly** – even in the Gents just before the speeches begin!

Deep breathing

1 Stand upright, relax your body and breathe in deeply.
2 Hold for ten seconds and slowly release.
3 Repeat five times.

Top tip
Use this time to think through your speech.

Stretching

1 Stretch up your arms as high as you can reach, standing on tiptoes.
2 Relax.
3 Stretch your arms as wide as you can.
4 Relax.
5 Repeat five times.

Scrunching and stretching your face

1 Scrunch up your face really tightly, pinching it in.
2 Relax.
3 Stretch your face as wide as possible, lifting your eyebrows and opening your mouth.
4 Relax.
5 Repeat five times.

Vocal warm-ups

These two-minute vocal exercises will help **release tension in your voice**. You can also perform them **anywhere**.

Yawning

1 Open your mouth wide and yawn loudly.
2 Repeat five times.

Humming

1 Hum one steady note, starting softly and growing louder.
2 Repeat, opening your mouth wide and allowing the sound out fully.
3 Repeat five times.

Lip and tongue mobility

1 Stick your tongue out and move it in large circles.
2 Repeat your favourite tongue twister.

● You can do your vocal warm-ups anywhere

7 Delivering your speech: the basics

An enjoyable performance

You've prepared your speech, and rehearsed it many times. You've got your cue cards ready and know the **main points** you are going to make. The only thing left to do is actually to make the speech.

There is little point in striving to write a wonderful speech and then failing to deliver it well. If it's not **enjoyable to listen to**, and your 'performance' isn't **enjoyable to watch**, your speech will be completely undermined.

On the other hand, everyone will love a well-delivered speech given in an **interesting way**, with **confidence**. It will be a **highlight** of the day and remembered for years to come.

This chapter tells you what you need to know about **delivering your speech**, including:

* putting your audience at ease
* setting the tone
* keeping to the script
* making eye contact
* avoiding fidgeting
* making sure you're heard
* the seven giveaways of a nervous speaker
* keeping the audience on your side.

A well-delivered speech will be a highlight of the day

● A happy audience

Putting your audience at ease

Everyone in the audience is willing you to do well, so avoid the temptation to tell them that you're not used to making speeches or that you're nervous, in the hope that it will:

* lower their expectations
* make you feel better
* break the ice.

It's a classic **trap** for the **unwary** and **inexperienced**, which instead will:

* make your audience uncomfortable
* make your audience nervous *for* you and *about* you
* undermine your speech.

Warning your guests that your speech won't be good is a great way to ensure that that's how they remember it – even if it was excellent. It's fine to be self-deprecating, as long as it doesn't detract from your purpose.

Setting the tone

Yours will be the first speech of the wedding, so it's crucial to establish the **right tone** – for you, and for the groom and best man who will come after you.

Your audience will probably be:

* expectant
* excited
* nervous on your behalf.

You will therefore need to:

1 put them at **ease** – if they relax and are confident in your abilities, it will **help you relax** and help them enjoy your speech

2 set an appropriate **tone** for the **content** of your speech, which might be:

✔ warm   ✔ delighted
✔ loving   ✔ joyful
✔ proud   ✔ relaxed

Top tip
Begin by saying something like, 'I'm so pleased to see so many of you here today.'

Keeping to the script

You've spent a lot of **time** and **effort** writing your speech – so **stick to it**! This will ensure that you:

✔ *say everything you wanted to say*
✔ *keep your speech tight and focused*
✔ *look and sound confident and in control*

✘ *don't say anything you may later regret*
✘ *don't dilute your speech with poor material*
✘ *don't go on too long.*

● A successful speech giver sticks to the script

> **'I only sound intelligent when there's a good script writer around.'**
> Christian Bale

Making eye contact

Establishing and maintaining **eye contact** with the members of your audience will mean you see them as individuals rather than just a sea of faces. It's one of the most important aspects of **good public speaking**.

Eye contact allows you to:

* **engage** with your audience
* establish a **rapport** with them
* make each guest feel **included**
* deliver your speech with **dynamism**.

It will also help you to:

* look confident
* look interested
* feel less nervous
* keep your head up!

Top tip

Make eye contact with one guest at a time, starting with someone at the back of the audience and delivering that part of your speech directly to them. Then move on to another guest.

Avoiding fidgeting

Any sort of fidgeting is both **annoying** to watch and **distracting**, and it will undermine what you're saying. Fidgeting is a natural reaction to being nervous and 'on show' but it must be **avoided** at all costs.

To prevent fidgeting, be aware of the ways in which you fidget – and the ways to combat them.

Type of fidgeting	Avoidance method
Shuffling feet	Keep feet firmly planted in one spot
Fiddling with rings or other jewellery	Keep hands on cue cards
Wringing hands	Keep hands apart
Running fingers through hair	Keep hands away from face and head
Shifting weight from one leg to the other	Keep weight centred
Rapid blinking	Concentrate on making eye contact

Making sure you're heard

There's no point in writing a great speech and **mastering** the subtleties of its delivery only to speak so quietly that you can't be heard. If you are using a microphone this will not be a problem; if not, you may be able to alter the **mechanics** of the venue to assist you. For example, you can:

* stand close to all the guests
* ensure that your audience is in front of you
* minimize background noise, by:
  » closing windows and doors
  » turning off air conditioning or heating.

In addition, to give yourself the **best chance of being heard**:

✔ *speak loudly and evenly, and address the back of the room*
✔ *speak slowly and clearly*

✔ *keep your head up*
✔ *take a deep breath before each sentence.*

Speak loudly and evenly

The seven giveaways of a nervous speaker

Controlling your nerves is important, but it's also important that you don't look nervous. Some of the most **common giveaways** to avoid are:

1 fidgeting
2 rapid swallowing
3 frequent coughing
4 nervous laughter
5 not lifting your head up
6 avoiding eye contact
7 speaking too quickly.

Starting your speech with a smile will help you – and your audience – relax.

> **Remember**
> If you appear nervous, your audience will be nervous – which in turn will make you even more nervous! If you appear confident, your audience will relax – and so will you.

● How *not* to look!

Keeping the audience on your side

You have a great advantage here – your audience will comprise friends and family who will be willing you to do well and **on your side** from the outset. Your task, then, is to **keep them there!**

Five key tips

1 **Keep smiling** – even if you feel it's going badly.
2 **Make eye contact** with as many people as possible.
3 Don't be tempted to rush – **take your time** and let your audience enjoy your speech.
4 **Keep to the script** – this will ensure that your material is first rate.
5 Try to sound as though you're enjoying yourself!

If you give your audience 'permission' to relax by appearing confident, they will be behind you all the way.

Your audience will be willing you to do well

8 Delivering your speech: advanced techniques

An outstanding speech

Once you've got the hang of the basics of **delivering your speech** it's time to move on to the more **advanced techniques**. Mastering these can make all the **difference** between a delivery that is **competent** and one that is **outstanding**.

Such outstanding delivery will gain the rapt attention – and admiration – of everyone in the room. Your speech will be thoroughly enjoyed on the day and **fondly remembered** for a long time to come.

● You'll feel fantastic afterwards!

It's possible to give a speech that will **enthral** your audience even if you have never spoken in public before. This chapter tells you all about the techniques you need to lift your speech to the **highest level**. It covers:

* dynamic delivery
* effective use of pauses and phrasing
* resisting the temptation to hurry
* overcoming mistakes
* varying your pace and pitch
* effective use of vocal tone and inflection.

Gain the rapt attention – and admiration – of everyone

Dynamic delivery

While you'll want your speech to be personal and unique to you, a dynamic delivery will hold your audience's attention and bring out the emotional responses you want. **Combining** the basic and advanced **techniques** for delivering your speech will enable you to present it in a manner that is:

* engaging
* sincere
* passionate
* inspirational
* memorable.

Top tip
Experiment with different combinations of techniques until you find your preferred style.

When you practise your speech, vary your style of delivery to discover the combination of techniques that:

* best suits your personality
* allows you to achieve the desired tone
* makes you feel most comfortable.

Using pauses and phrasing

Pauses help to break up the pattern of your speech so that it's **pleasingly phrased**. You want to avoid giving the impression that you are saying one long, **never-ending sentence**. Pauses will also:

1 allow your audience to **take in** what you've said
2 give your audience **time** to **laugh** – or to **reflect**
3 build **expectation**
4 **break up** a long story
5 prevent you from **gabbling**
6 allow you to **prepare** for the next part of your speech.

Top tip
If you wish to inject **humour** into your speech, try using a **'pregnant pause'** – pausing at the end of a phrase to build **suspense** before a **punch line**.

'The right word may be effective, but no word was ever as effective as a rightly timed pause.'
Mark Twain

Resisting the temptation to hurry

If you're unused to public speaking, it's natural to be tempted to rush your speech. This is almost always the result of **nerves** and the **pressure** of the occasion. However, try to avoid it because rushing:

* makes you sound nervous
* makes it difficult for the audience to hear you
* makes it difficult for the audience to keep up.

Just before you stand up to start speaking (and not too obviously), let out several deep, slow, **controlled sighs** to fill your lungs completely with air. This will help you to:

* start with a good strong voice
* maintain a consistent flow of air
* slow down your heart rate
* distract yourself from being nervous.

Top tip
Write the word 'pause' at intervals through your notes or cue cards.

Overcoming mistakes

During the course of your speech it's highly likely that you will make a mistake (or several!), especially if you are unused to public speaking. Mistakes in themselves **don't matter**; what **matters** is how you **deal** with them.

Common mistakes	How to overcome them
Stumbling over words	Just repeat them, more slowly
Losing your place in the 'script'	Take your time to find it again
Never lifting your head	Make regular eye contact
Speaking too quietly	Deliver every word to the back of the room
Panicking	Take a deep breath and carry on

'Experience is simply the name we give our mistakes.'
Oscar Wilde

Varying pace and pitch

The most interesting speech soon loses its appeal if delivered in a monotone. Varying pace and pitch provides **dramatic effect and emphasis**, helping to maintain your audience's interest.

Pace

Varying the pace of your delivery also helps you **underline** what you are saying.

Remember
Whatever pace you're aiming for, go more slowly than you think you should. Halve the speed you think feels right, and halve it again if you're nervous.

Speak slowly when you:

* are saying something serious
* need to be solemn
* want to add gravity to your message.

Speak more quickly when you:

* want to keep your message light-hearted
* are using humour
* are saying something upbeat.

Pitch

You can vary the pitch of your voice to help convey your message.

Use a low pitch to help convey:

* seriousness
* solemnity
* genuineness.

Use a high pitch to help convey:

* lightness
* humour
* joy.

Remember

Your voice may be naturally high or low pitched, so be aware of this when varying your pitch.

● You might prefer to practise in private

Effective use of tone

The tone of your voice imparts the **underlying message** implicit in what you're saying, regardless of the content. It's important to be aware of your tone since it can convey an unwanted or unintended sentiment.

By using tone, you can colour your voice with **emotion** or **feelings**, such as:

Don't talk to me in that tone of voice!

* happiness
* sadness
* pride
* warmth
* joy.

This will enable you to convey your feelings quickly and openly, and actively **support your message**.

Top tip
Before you deliver each section of your speech, try thinking of an occasion when you felt the emotion you wish to convey.

94

Effective use of inflection

The inflection in your voice means the **rising** and **falling** patterns you create in your speech. Using inflection is important because it will:

* help paint a picture of what you're saying
* introduce vocal variety
* keep your audience interested
* underline the most important parts.

By **modulating** your voice, you can help to make your manner of speaking interesting to listen to, and deliver the content of your speech with **maximum impact**.

Make your manner of speaking interesting

Top tip
Avoid the dreaded 'rising inflection'! Unless you are asking or posing a question, always make sure that you bring your voice down at the end of a sentence.

9 Pitfalls and pratfalls – and how to avoid them

Potential hazards

Unless public speaking is your profession, you're likely to encounter a number of **unfamiliar situations** on the big day. Even when you have practised and prepared in order to give yourself the best possible chance of everything going smoothly, you will still be susceptible to **potential hazards** ready to wrongfoot the unwary.

'Forewarned is forearmed': by getting to know these pitfalls and pratfalls now, you can plan for all eventualities.

● Be on guard for 'banana skin' moments!

You want to make a speech of which you can be **proud**, free of blunders that might irritate or offend your audience. Likewise, you want to remain **unfazed** if something unforeseen happens during your speech. This chapter tells you how to avoid the most **common pitfalls**, which are:

* trying to ad-lib
* allowing interruptions
* straying from the subject
* becoming overwhelmed
* using too many props
* relying on technology
* inappropriate material
* humour overload.

Forewarned is forearmed

Trying to ad-lib

Ad-libbing – making **unscripted** remarks **off the cuff** – is a skill best left to the professionals. They make it look easy, but don't be fooled: it's an incredibly difficult art to master and you're almost always better off sticking to the script. If your ad-lib is not brilliant, it can all too easily fall flat.

The biggest **danger** with ad-libbing is that, in the **heat of the moment**, under the pressure to perform and filled with adrenalin, you may say something you wish you hadn't.

You're better off sticking to the script

Remember
It only takes an **unguarded second** to say the **wrong** thing, but you might **regret** it for a long time.

Allowing interruptions

Friendly heckling during wedding speeches is common. Usually it's because:

* the heckler is nervous:
  » for you
  » for themselves (if they are speaking next)
* the heckler thinks it will help you by:
  » providing a friendly voice
  » drawing focus
  » adding to your speech.

● Don't let hecklers drown you out

101

Top tip

Beware the snowball effect! If you allow one person to interrupt your speech, others might quickly jump on the bandwagon and, before you know it, you have been made redundant and left looking awkward.

Straying from the subject

If you have carefully written your speech and practised it, you are far better off keeping to it. **Wandering off** at a tangent will at best:

* **dilute** the **content** of your speech
* lose the **focus** of your **message**
* make you seem **less competent**.

At worst it will:

* have **little** to do with the **wedding**
* appear **selfish** and **rude**
* make your speech **too long**.

By sticking to the subject and **keeping to the script**, you will know what you're saying, and you'll appear confident and in control.

> **'It's better to keep your mouth shut and give the impression that you're stupid than to open it and remove all doubt.'**
> Rami Belson

Becoming overwhelmed

Despite diligent practice and preparation, you won't be able to replicate exactly what it will be like on the day because of:

* the attendant **emotions** you'll experience
* the **size** of the gathering
* the **atmosphere** and sense of occasion.

So there's always the possibility that you'll feel overwhelmed. In order to prevent this:

* take several **deep breaths** before you begin
* have a **glass of water** to hand, to:
  » keep your mouth from drying
  » give you time to compose yourself.

Top tip
Avoid drinking alcohol to calm your nerves – it doesn't work and leaves you less in control.

Using too many props

While a good way to add variety to your speech is to use props, beware of using too many.

Props can be used to great effect to:	However, too many props can:
add humour	make your speech cluttered
create drama	slow you down
invoke nostalgia.	draw emphasis from what you're saying.

Props should therefore be kept to a **minimum** and used **sparingly**.
Only include them if they are:

1 completely relevant
2 entirely appropriate
3 suitable to the occasion and the venue
4 going to complement your speech –
   not undermine it.

Top tip
Check out the venue in advance to determine where to keep props until you need them.

Relying on technology

You may wish to employ some form of **technology** in your speech to add variety, create intrigue or just to give you a break. Some common examples are:

* **audio** recordings (for example, the bride's favourite childhood band)
* **video** recordings
* **slide** presentations.

However, all technology is susceptible to **Murphy's Law**: 'If it can go wrong, it will go wrong'! So always make sure you have a **back-up plan**.

Technology **must** be:

* relevant
* audible/visible to everyone
* ready to start and finish instantly.

Technology **must not** be:

* the **mainstay** of your speech
* **generic** (for example, copied straight from the internet)
* **relied upon**!

Inappropriate material

Your speech can quickly go horribly wrong if you include anything inappropriate. This can be material that is:

* risqué or lewd
* overtly political or radical
* likely to cause offence to specific guests.

Your wedding speech is not a time to take risks. **Err on the side of caution** and, if you're unsure about including something, leave it out. In particular, don't use this as an opportunity to:

* score points or gloat
* tell embarrassing stories
* mention exes
* use foul or abusive language.

'The real art of conversation is...to leave unsaid the wrong thing at the tempting moment.'

Dorothy Nevill

Humour overload

It may be tempting to crack **jokes** or relate a succession of **amusing anecdotes**, despite knowing that you should **restrict** them. This is because:

* getting the audience laughing relaxes them and you
* they are great time-fillers
* they will keep everyone entertained
* it means you don't have to say anything more demanding.

However, it's best to use them **sparingly** and with **precision** so that they:

* stand out
* add variety
* aren't all there is!

By varying your material, you'll be able to vary your delivery and keep your audience's interest.

Top tip
Aim to make them laugh *and* cry: try to get a good mixture of elements that includes humour, but also seriousness, pathos and joy.

10 Useful resources

Borrowing material

Your speech should be unique and personal to you and the happy couple, but that doesn't mean you shouldn't **borrow** material to supplement yours. After all, with the **wit and wisdom** of so many famous fathers of the bride on which to draw, you're bound to find something which encapsulates **exactly what you want to say**, and says it superbly.

And, thanks to the **internet**, research has never been easier.

● A pithy, witty quote can be a brilliant resource

There is a wide range of possible material that you could add to your speech. Make sure you choose something **suitable** for your particular circumstances and something that you know will **appeal** to your audience, and especially the bride and groom.

This chapter offers just a tiny selection of what is available, including:

* quotes about marriage
* quotes about love
* humorous quotes
* jokes
* toasts
* poems.

**Thanks to the internet, research
has never been easier**

Quotes about marriage

A good quote can provide an excellent **route into your speech**, or it can be used to **underline a point** you wish to make.

'Marriage is the perfection
of what love aimed at,
ignorant of what it sought.'
Ralph Waldo Emerson

'To keep your marriage brimming,
with love in the wedding cup,
whenever you're wrong, admit it;
whenever you're right, shut up.'
Ogden Nash

'Marriage has some thorns,
but celibacy has no roses.'
Vernon McClellan

'The best friend is likely
to acquire the best wife,
because a good marriage is based
on the talent for friendship.'
Friedrich Nietzsche

'Marriage is the golden ring in
a chain whose beginning is a glance
and whose ending is Eternity.'
Kahlil Gibran

'Only choose in marriage
a man whom you would choose
as a friend if he were a woman.'
Joseph Joubert

'Marriage is like a pair of shears,
oft times working in opposite
directions, but punishing anyone
who comes between them.'
Sydney Smith

'Happy marriages begin
when we marry the ones we love,
and they blossom when we love
the ones we marry.'
Tom Mullen

'A good marriage is one which
allows for change and growth in
the individuals and in the way
they express their love.'
Pearl S. Buck

'Two such as you
with such a master speed
Cannot be parted nor be swept away
From one another once you are agreed
That life is only life forevermore
Together wing to wing and oar to oar.'
Robert Frost

'Happy marriage is the greatest
wealth a man can possess,
and one that a peasant can have
as easily as a king.'
Douglas Carlton Abrams

'Don't marry the person
you think you can live with;
marry only the individual
you think you can't live without.'
James C. Dobson

Quotes about love

'To love someone deeply
gives you strength.
Being loved by someone deeply
gives you courage.'

Lao Tzu

'Love is not blind –
it sees more and not less,
but because it sees more
it is willing to see less.'

Will Moss

'Remember that
happiness is a way of travel,
not a destination.'

Roy Goodman

'Love takes off masks that
we fear we cannot live without
and know we cannot live within.'

James A. Baldwin

'Nothing is lovely
without love itself,
and nothing is lovelier
than love itself.'

Devan Penegar

'There is only one happiness in life,
to love and be loved.'

George Sand

Humorous quotes

'Every mother generally hopes
that her daughter will snag
a better husband than
she managed to do –
but she's certain that
her boy will never get
as great a wife
as his father did.'

Anon.

'Why does a woman work
for ten years to change
a man's habits,
and then complain
he's not the man she married?'

Barbara Streisand

'Being a husband is
a whole-time job.
That is why so many
husbands fail.
They cannot give their
entire attention to it.'

Arnold Bennett

'When a newly married
couple smiles,
everyone knows why.
When a ten-year married
couple smiles,
everyone wonders why.'

Anon.

Jokes

Jokes can make great **icebreakers**, such as:

*'Marriage is an important commitment,
so much so that you need a mortgage
to pay for it!'*

*'There are only two times in a man's life
when he can't understand a woman –
before marriage and after marriage.'*

About your new son-in-law:

*'We call him the exorcist in our house.
Every time he comes around,
he rids us of all the spirits!'*

*'The man who says his wife can't take a joke,
forgets that she took him.'*

Oscar Wilde

● Remember your audience
– jokes must be funny but
never smutty!

116

Toasts

Your speech should be rounded off with a toast, which can be either **serious** or **humorous**. Here are some examples:

'A toast to sweethearts: "May all sweethearts become married couples, and may all married couples remain sweethearts."'

'Marriage is like wine – it gets better with age.'

'The most effective way to remember your wedding anniversary is to forget once.'

'The sum which two married people owe to one another defies calculation. It is an infinite debt, which can only be discharged through eternity.'

Remember
Whatever toast you use it should **finish** with, '**Ladies and Gentlemen**, please join me in **a toast to the bride and groom**!'

Poems

Reading a **poem** is a great way to add **variety** to your speech. It will also give you a **pause** from directly addressing the audience. Poetry is a **beautiful** way to express yourself **succinctly,** and since the subject of **'love'** has inspired poets for centuries you're spoilt for choice.

Here are two examples:

To Be One With Each Other

What greater thing is there for two human souls
than to feel that they are joined together to strengthen
each other in all labour, to minister to each other in all sorrow,
to share with each other in all gladness,
to be one with each other in the silent unspoken memories?

George Eliot

Sonnet 116

Let me not to the marriage of true minds
Admit impediments. Love is not love
Which alters when it alteration finds,
Or bends with the remover to remove:
Oh, no! It is an ever-fixed mark.
That looks on tempests and is never shaken;
It is the star to every wandering bark,
Whose worth's unknown, although his height be taken.
Love's not Time's fool, though rosy lips and cheeks
Within his bending sickle's compass come;
Love alters not with his brief hours and weeks,
But bears it out even to the edge of doom.
If this be error and upon me proved,
I never writ, nor no man ever loved.

William Shakespeare